First World War
and Army of Occupation
War Diary
France, Belgium and Germany

38 DIVISION
Divisional Troops
Royal Army Medical Corps
Divisional Field Ambulance Workshop Unit
1 December 1915 - 31 March 1916

WO95/2550/2

The Naval & Military Press Ltd
www.nmarchive.com
Published in association with The National Archives

Published by

The Naval & Military Press Ltd

Unit 10 Ridgewood Industrial Park,

Uckfield, East Sussex,

TN22 5QE England

Tel: +44 (0) 1825 749494

www.naval-military-press.com

www.nmarchive.com

This diary has been reprinted in facsimile from the original. Any imperfections are inevitably reproduced and the quality may fall short of modern type and cartographic standards.

© **Crown Copyright**
Images reproduced by permission of The National Archives, London, England, 2015.

Contents

Document type	Place/Title	Date From	Date To
Miscellaneous	WO95/2550/2 Divisional Field Ambulance Workshop Unit		
Heading	38th Division Medical 38th Fd Amb. W'shop Unit Dec 1915-Mar 1916		
Heading	38th F.A.W.U. Vol I. Dec 1915-Mar 16		
Heading	War Diary Of 38th Div Ambulance Workshop Unit. From Dec 1st 1915 To Dec 31st 1915		
War Diary	Lingy-Les-Aire	01/12/1915	01/12/1915
War Diary	Aire	01/12/1915	03/12/1915
War Diary	Quiestede	04/12/1915	09/12/1915
War Diary	Moulin-Les-Comte	09/12/1915	21/12/1915
War Diary	Calonne-Sur-Lys	22/12/1915	31/12/1915
Heading	38th F.A.W.U. Jan. 1916-Feb 1916		
Heading	38th F.A.W.U. Vol. 2		
War Diary	Calonne-Sur-Lys	01/01/1916	24/01/1916
War Diary	Lestrem	25/01/1916	31/01/1916
Heading	38th F.A.W.U. Vol 3		
War Diary	Lestrem	01/02/1916	19/02/1916
War Diary	Locon	19/02/1916	29/02/1916
Heading	38th Div. W.U. March 1916		
War Diary	Locon	01/03/1916	31/03/1916

WO95/2550/2

Divisional Field Ambulance
Workshop Unit

38TH DIVISION
MEDICAL

38TH FD AMB. W'SHOP UNIT
DEC 1915 – MAR 1916

Late Meerut

F.

38th F.A.W.U.
Vol: I

Dec 1915

1

Mei '16

CONFIDENTIAL.

WAR DIARY.

OF

38th Div Ambulance Workshop Unit.

From Dec 1st 1915 To Dec 31st 1915.

WAR DIARY or INTELLIGENCE SUMMARY

(Erase heading not required.)

Army Form C. 2118.

38th Div. Ambulance Workshop Unit.

Place	Date	Hour	Summary of Events and Information	Remarks and references to Appendices
LINGY-LES-AIRE	1/12/15	2.15 pm	Under instructions received from D.D. of S.T. 1st Army the Unit consisting of Workshop and 21 Ambulances proceeded to Aire to report to D.D. of S.T.	
AIRE	"	4 P.M.	Arrived at AIRE, Workshop & Ambulances parked in road on outskirts of town. O.C. proceeded to D.D. of S.T. office to report arrival. Received instructions to wait for further orders.	
"	2/12/15		Remained at AIRE. Ambulances were cleaned etc.	
		5.30 p.m	Received orders from D.D./B.T. 1st Army Letter No S.T. 2111 to proceed with Unit to QUIESTÈDE, and to report arrival by wire to H.Q. XIth Corps.	
"	3/12/15	9.30 a.m	Unit moved off from AIRE arriving at QUIESTEDE at 11.A.M. Workshop and AMBULANCES were parked in yard of large farm.	
QUIESTÈDE	4/12/15		All cars were cleaned and thoroughly inspected and repaired where necessary.	
"	5/12/15		Work on Cars carried on.	
	6/12/15		Work on Cars carried on.	
	7/12/15		Inspection and work on Ambulances completed. Received orders from H.Q. 38th Division to proceed with Ambulances to CLARQUES and report to O.C. 129th Field Ambulance.	

WAR DIARY or INTELLIGENCE SUMMARY.

(Erase heading not required.)

Army Form C. 2118.

38th Div Ambulance Workshop Unit

Place	Date	Hour	Summary of Events and Information	Remarks and references to Appendices
QUIESTÈDE	8/12/15	9 am	Proceeded with Ambulances to CLARQUES. Reported to O.C. 129th Field Ambulance and handed over 7 Ambulances. Then proceeded with remainder of Ambulances to GLOMENGHEM and reported to O.C. 130th Field Ambulance and handed over 7 Ambulances. Proceeded to ST QUENTIN and reported to O.C. 131st Field Ambulance and handed over 7 Ambulances. Receive instruction from A.D.M.S. to go with Workshop to GLOMENGHEM tomorrow.	
"	9/2/15		Proceed to GLOMENGHEM to get billets & find suitable Workshop site. This is a very small village with no suitable place for WORKSHOP and nearly every billet occupied by the personnel of 130th Field Ambulance. Proceed to MOULIN-LE-COMTE and find good place for Workshop. Then proceed to H.Q. Division and report and obtain permission to proceed with Workshop to MOULIN-LE-COMTE. Return to QUIESTÈDE. On arrival find Officer from 46th Div Sup Ammunition Park who informs me that he has come to transfer his WOLSELEY Car to me and to take SUNBEAM Car in place under authority of D.D. of S.T. 1st ARMY. The transfer is effected then and there. Then proceed with Workshop to MOULIN-LE-COMTE arriving there at 5-30 P.M. Weather very wet. Received instructions from D.D. of S.T. to transfer 2 DOUGLAS Motor Cycles to 46th	

WAR DIARY or INTELLIGENCE SUMMARY

Army Form C. 2118.

38th DIV. AMBULANCE WORKSHOP UNIT

Place	Date	Hour	Summary of Events and Information	Remarks and references to Appendices
MOULIN-LE-COMTE	9/12/15	7.30am	To 46th Div F.A.W.U. in exchange for 2 TRIUMPH Motor cycles. and to transfer 2 DOUGLAS motor cycles to the 46th Divisional Cavalry in exchange for 1 TRIUMPH motor cycle and 1 RUDGE. Report to A.D.M.S. by letter that move has been completed giving location.	
"	10/12/15		Received letter from D.D. of S.&T. informing me to be prepared to transfer 12 SUNBEAM GIFT AMBULANCES to 1st Div INDIAN Cavalry and 3 SUNBEAM Gift AMBULANCES to 2nd Div INDIAN Cavalry. date to be notified later. O.C. reported personally to A.D.M.S. and discussed arrangements for transferring Ambulances. The transfer of 2 Douglas M/cs to 46 Div. F.A.W.U. was effected & 2 TRIUMPH M/cs received.	
"	11/12/15		Transfer of 2 DOUGLAS M/cs to 46th Div Cavalry (Yorkshire Hussars) was effected and 1 TRIUMPH and 1 RUDGE motorcycle received. These machines were accepted under protest as both of them were unfit for service and were deficient in equipment.	
"	12/12/15		O.C. went to STEENBECQUE to see O.C. 38th Div Supply COLUMN re sending the 2 unserviceable M/cs in for replacement.	
"	13/12/15		Received orders from H.Q. 38th Div to effect transfer of SUNBEAM AMBULANCES to the 1st & 2nd INDIAN Cavalry Divisions on the 14th and 15th insts respectively.	

WAR DIARY or INTELLIGENCE SUMMARY

Army Form C. 2118.

Instructions regarding War Diaries and Intelligence Summaries are contained in F. S. Regs., Part II. and the Staff Manual respectively. Title pages will be prepared in manuscript.

(Erase heading not required.) 38th Div Ambulance Workshop Unit.

Place	Date	Hour	Summary of Events and Information	Remarks and references to Appendices
MOULIN-LE-COMTE	13/12/15		No. M/S 566 Pte Bicknell G.F. was taken on the strength as Electrician to complete establishment being transferred from 38th Div Supply Column.	
"	14/12/15	9-30 AM	Proceeded with Convoy of 12 SUNBEAM Ambulances to LE QUESNOY arriving there at 3-30 PM. Handed over Cars to O.C. 1st Div Indian Cavalry and received 12. 16/20 hp WOLSELEY cars in exchange. Then returned with Convoy of WOLSELEY Ambulances to MOULIN-LE-COMTE arriving at 2 AM on the 15th inst.	
"	15/12/15	10 AM	Proceeded with 3 SUNBEAM Ambulances to OISEMONT arriving there at 4 PM. Handed over Cars to O.C. 2nd Div Indian Cavalry. F.A.W.U. ~~...~~ On arrival was informed by O.C. 2nd Indian Cavalry Div F.A.W.U. that WOLSELEY AMBULANCES had been despatched that morning under instructions received, to AIRE to report to O.C. TROOPS SUPPLY COLUMN 1st ARMY. Returned to MOULIN-LE-COMTE arriving back at 1-30 AM on the 16th inst.	
"	16/12/15	9-30 AM	Reported to O.C. 1st ARMY TROOPS Supply Column and took over 3 24/30 hp WOLSELEY Ambulances	
"	17-12-15		Nothing of note to record.	
"	18/12/15		Nothing of note to record	
"	19/12/15		Nothing of note to record.	

WAR DIARY or INTELLIGENCE SUMMARY

Army Form C. 2118.

(Erase heading not required.) 38th DW. Ambulance. Workshop Unit.

Place	Date	Hour	Summary of Events and Information	Remarks and references to Appendices
MOULIN-LE-COMTE	20/12/15		Received instructions from A.D.M.S. that the Unit would move on the 21st inst to CALONNE. O.C. proceeded to CALONNE to find WORKSHOP SITE and Billets.	
"	21/12/15	1 P.M.	WORKSHOP Unit moved off arriving at CALONNE at 4.P.M. WORKSHOP took up position in FARM yard of farm situated at Q.9.d.8.8. Sheet 36.A.	
CALONNE-SUR-LYS	22/12/15		Nothing of note to record.	
"	23/12/15		Nothing of note to record.	
"	24/12/15		Nothing of note to record.	
"	25/12/15		Kept as a general holiday for all ranks.	
		3 P.M.	Received wire that a Divisional Train Car was broken down at GLOMENGHEM. O.C. proceeded with breakdown lorry and found car with front wheel off. Temporarily effected repair & brought car in arriving back at 9.P.M.	
"	26/12/15		Nothing of note to report.	
"	27/12/15		N.C.O's & men proceeded to MERVILLE to attend Concert by the 19th DIVISION FOLLIES. The performance was much appreciated.	
"	28/12/15		Nothing of note to record.	
"	29/12/15		Received letter from A.D.M.S. to effect that in future the designation of this Unit is to be	

WAR DIARY or ~~INTELLIGENCE SUMMARY~~.

Army Form C. 2118.

38th Div. Ambulance Workshop Unit

Place	Date	Hour	Summary of Events and Information	Remarks and references to Appendices
CALONNE-SUR-LYS	29/12/15		*to be* Div. Ambulance Workshop and not Div Field Ambulance Workshop Unit which designation he rules to be irregular. M2/052381 Corp Rogers W. proceeded on 7 day leave to England.	
CALONNE-SUR-LYS	30/12/15		Nothing of note to record.	
"	31/12/15		Nothing of note to record.	

S.H.Lambert 2/Lt A.S.C.
O.C. 38th Div Ambulance Workshop

38th Y.A.W.U.

Jan. 1916.
Feb. 1916

38th Paw. U.
Vol. 2

WAR DIARY
or
~~INTELLIGENCE SUMMARY~~
(Erase heading not required.)

Army Form C. 2118.

38th Div. Ambulance Workshop Unit.

Place	Date	Hour	Summary of Events and Information	Remarks and references to Appendices
CALONNE-SUR-LYS	1-1-16		Nothing of note to record.	
"	2-1-16		No m/z 080077 Pt Blackwell H.R. proceeded on 7 days leave to England.	
"	3-1-16		Received 2 Douglas Motor Cycles from "B" Squadron Yorkshire Hussars under instructions from D.D. of S.T. Both machines in bad condition.	
"	4-1-16		Nothing of note to record.	
"	5-1-16		No m/z 052381 Cpl Rogers V. returned from leave.	
"	6-1-16		Recd Circular memo re submitting names of officers who wished to transfer to R.F.C.	
"	7-1-16		Requested by A.D.M.S. to examine Pt Llewellyn R.A.M.C. of 129th Field Ambulance as to his capabilities as a motorcyclist. Tested and passed.	
"	8-1-16		No m/z 080077 Pt Blackwell H.R. returned from leave.	
"	9-1-16		Examined No 48615 Pt Roberts J.H. R.A.M.C as a motor cyclist. Passed.	
"	10-1-16		No m/z 102795 Pt Jolly sent to Hospital for medical examination. Received medical certificate that he is suffering from neurasthenia & recommended for a rest.	
"	11-1-16		Nothing of note to record.	
"	12-1-16		Nothing of note to record.	
"	13-1-16		Nothing of note to record.	

WAR DIARY or ~~INTELLIGENCE SUMMARY~~

(Erase heading not required.)

38th Div Ambulance Workshop Unit

Army Form C. 2118.

Place	Date	Hour	Summary of Events and Information	Remarks and references to Appendices
CALONNE-SUR-LYS	14-1-16		The following A.S.C. details arrived from Div Supply Column to complete establishment of A.S.C. personnel attached to Field Ambulances:- M2/115186 Pte Scholey S.E., M2/133889 Pte Maltby J., M2/047525 Pte Foley E.P., M2/053713 Pte Gardner M., M4/060892 Pte Wallis G., DM3/134622 Pte Walker R. These men were distributed as follows:- To 129 F.A. Pte Scholey S.E. and Pte Maltby J. To 130 F.A. Pte Gardner M. and Pte Foley E.P. To 131st F.A. Pte Wallis G. and Pte Walker R.	
"	15-1-16		Submitted name of No M2/102795 Pte Jolly J.C. with medical certificate that he is suffering from Neurasthenia for grant of special leave.	
"	16-1-16		No M1/5895 Pte Lambert E.N. proceeded on 7 days leave.	
		11 AM	Received notification that Ambulance No 1550 had broken down near ROBECQUE. Proceeded with lorry and brought car in.	
		3.30 pm	Received orders to proceed to A.D.M.S. office to discuss alterations to Ford Ambulances.	
"	17-1-16		No M2/2110 Pte Fitzgerald proceeded on 7 days leave to England. Received orders from ADMS to proceed with Ford alterations.	
"	18-1-16		D.D.M.S. XIth Corps and A.D.M.S. 38th Div visited Workshop. The alterations	

WAR DIARY

Army Form C. 2118.

(Intelligence Summary struck through)

38th Div Ambulance Workshop Unit

Place	Date	Hour	Summary of Events and Information	Remarks and references to Appendices
Calonne-sur-Lys	18-1-16		The alterations to Ford Ambulances were discussed. The O.C. reported that the instructions received re the alterations were insufficient and expressed his opinion that further instructions would be forthcoming from the D.D. of S.T. in due course.	
"	19-1-16		Received Circular Memorandum from D.D. of S.T. No S.T. 171/16 giving full particulars of alterations to Ford Cars with sketches.	
"	20-1-16		Having been informed by A.D.M.S. that the H.2s Div were moving to Lestrem and that the 19th Div F.A.W.U. were at present lighting the H.2s Chateau, it was desired that this Unit should take over from the 19th F.A.W.U. and continue with the lighting when the Divisions changed.	
"	21-1-16		Received instructions from A.D.M.S. that the Unit would move to Lestrem on the 24th inst. and take over from the 19th Div. F.A.W.U.	
"	22-2-16		Proceeded to Lestrem to see O.C. 19th Div F.A.W.U. re taking over from him on the 24th inst.	
"	23-2-16		Proceeded to Lestrem to make final billeting arrangements.	
"	24-1-16	9.30 a.m.	Spare Lorry proceeded to Lestrem with Advance party to take over from 19th Div. F.A.W.U.	
		11 a.m.	Store Lorry moved off to Lestrem, becomes ditched at 2.22.6.4. Sheet 36.A. This is	

WAR DIARY ~~or INTELLIGENCE SUMMARY~~

(Erase heading not required.)

Army Form C. 2118.

38th. Div. Ambulance Workshop Unit.

Place	Date	Hour	Summary of Events and Information	Remarks and references to Appendices
CALONNE-SUR-LYS	24-1-16		This is a very bad road, with just the crown of the road metalled, either side being thick soft mud with no bottom. Lorry was leaning over at a dangerous angle. Proceeded to jack up lorry by means of 2, 4 ton jacks, at the same time packing up back wheel gradually. By this means lorry was raised to an upright position, and then driven back to crown of road.	
LESTREM	25-1-16		Wiring Head Quarters of Division Chateau for Electric light. Pte. M/y 5895 Pte. LAMBERT. E.V. and No. M/y 2110 Pte. FITZGERALD. J. returned from leave.	
"	26-1-16		Rec'd Letter from D.D. of S.&T. letter ST. 210/16. Re M.T. STORES eg that in future no "Demands Noted" telegrams would be sent by O.C. Advanced M.T. Depot as heretofore.	
"	27-1-16		Nothing of note to record.	
"	28-1-16		Nothing of note to record.	
"	29-1-16		Received from D.H.Q. Table of new maps to be used.	
"	30-1-16		Nothing of note to record.	
"	31-1-16		Nothing of note to record.	

St Lambert s/Lt A.S.C.
O.C. 38th (Welsh) Division Ambulance Workshop.

38½ P. a. W. v
fol. 3

WAR DIARY or INTELLIGENCE SUMMARY.

Army Form C. 2118.

38th Div. Ambulance Workshop Unit.

Place	Date	Hour	Summary of Events and Information	Remarks and references to Appendices
LESTREM	1-2-16		OC. applied to A.D.M.S. for grant of leave to proceed to England.	
"	2-2-16		Nothing of note to record.	
"	3-2-16		OC. proceeded on leave to England.	
"	4-2-16		Received from A.D.M.S letter re Cow lights fitted to Ambulances. Memo on this subject from the D.M.S.	
"	5-2-16		Austin workshop Engine taken down. Fitted new shaft for intermediate timing pinion. Fitted baffle plates to crankcase.	
"	6-2-16		Nothing of note to report	
"	7-2-16		Pte Jolly J.C. admitted to Hpl.	
"	8-2-16		Work on Austin Engine completed. Received circular Memo from D of T with reference to servants.	
"	9-2-16		Nothing of note to Report.	
"	10-2-16		Received Memo from DOST re air hardened gears for Daimler cars.	
"	11-2-16		Nothing of note to report.	
"	12-2-16		Received Memo from A.G. office asking for nominal rolls of artificers serving in this unit	
"	13-2-16		Pte Jolly J.C. discharged from Hpl & reported for duty.	

for O.C.

WAR DIARY or ~~INTELLIGENCE SUMMARY~~

(Erase heading not required.)

Army Form C. 2118.

Instructions regarding War Diaries and Intelligence Summaries are contained in F. S. Regs., Part II. and the Staff Manual respectively. Title pages will be prepared in manuscript.

38 Div Ambulance Workshop. Unit.

Place	Date	Hour	Summary of Events and Information	Remarks and references to Appendices
LESTREM.	13-2-16		O.C. returned to Duty from leave.	
"	14-2-16		Received letter from D.D of S.+T. re fitting of Low LIGHTS to Ambulances. Reported at A.D.M.S. Office and discussed matter of fitting LOW LIGHTS to Ambulances.	
"	15-2-16		Lt Jolly. J.C. proceeded to England on leave.	
"	16-2-16		Received Operation Order from A.D.M.S. to be ready to move to LOCON on the 19th inst.	
"	17-2-16		Proceeded to LOCON with CAMP COMMANDANT to see proposed WORKSHOP pitch and to arrange BILLETS. O.C. 35 Div F.A.W.U. called to arrange to take over from this Unit on the 19th inst.	
"	18-2-16		D.H.Qrs. moved to LOCON 35 D.H.Qrs. came into the H.Q. CHATEAU at LESTREM.	
"	19-2-16	7-15	Advance party moved off to LOCON on DAIMLER LORRY with STORES.	
		9-15	Remainder of Unit moved off arriving at LOCON at 11 AM. Took up Workshop position in yard behind D.H.Qrs. Ground very soft & muddy. In moving into position rear wheel of STORE LORRY sank into old refuse PIT which had been loosely filled in and covered with slag. LORRY was got out without difficulty. Received letter from A.D.M.S. re Order from D of T that FODEN LORRY DISINFECTOR will in future be maintained by this Unit, the O.C. being responsible	

WAR DIARY

~~INTELLIGENCE~~ SUMMARY.

(Erase heading not required.) 38. DIV. AMBULANCE. WORKSHOP. UNIT.

Army Form C. 2118.

Place	Date	Hour	Summary of Events and Information	Remarks and references to Appendices
LOCON.	19/2/16		responsible/ for the maintenance, supervision, cleaning, and, repair of same. German Aeroplanes dropped a bomb in a field close to D.H.Q at about 11-30 PM it being a beautiful bright moonlight night. Other Bombs were dropped on BETHUNE.	
LOCON	20-2-16		Unit engaged in clearing mud in WORKSHOP yard & putting up Tarpaulin etc.	
		3.P.M.	About 22 English AEROPLANES passed over LOCON presumably on a raid. Started to wire H.Q. Offices for ELECTRIC LIGHT.	
		10 PM.	GAS ALARM men turned out of billet and donned respirators.	
"	21-2-16		Received C.R.O. No 211 dated Feb 20th to the effect that WEEKLY REPORTS of the estimated mileage of CARS & AMBULANCES and of the exact quantities of PETROL and LUBRICANTS issued, are to be forwarded to the DD of S&T by UNITS direct each Saturday.	
"	22-2-16		Lt Bicknell G.F. proceeded to England on 7 days leave. Fall of snow in the morning, weather generally severe. Wiring of H.Qs offices completed. Received ARMSTRONG HUT for use as office, no office accommodation available in village.	

WAR DIARY or INTELLIGENCE SUMMARY.

(Erase heading not required.)

Army Form C. 2118.

38th Div. Ambulance Workshop Unit.

Place	Date	Hour	Summary of Events and Information	Remarks and references to Appendices
LOCON.	23-2-16		Severe weather continues much snow.	
"	24-2-16		Severe weather continues.	
"	25-2-16		Further fall of snow.	
"	26-2-16		O.C. proceeded to AIRE to report to D.D. of S+T.	
"	27-2-16		Received telegram from D.H.Q. "ADOPT THAW PRECAUTIONS 3 DAYS" General thaw set in.	
"	28-2-16		2 Postal LORRIES from Div Supply COLUMN attached to the Unit at request of C.O. Supply Column for 3 days during THAW PRECAUTIONS.	
"	29-2-16		Much Aeroplane activity 8 German machines flew over LOCON in the morning, one of which was brought down by 2 of our machines 2 MILES west of MERVILLE. It is reported that 2 other German machines were brought down also.	
		9-30	Gas Alarm men were warned but was only practice alarm.	

S H Lambert 2/Lt A.S.C.
O.C. 38th Div Amb. Workshop.

March 1916.

38th Divn. M. M.

COMMITTEE FOR THE
MEDICAL HISTORY OF THE WAR
Date 26 JUN 1916

MARCH. 1916.   Vol 4

WAR DIARY or INTELLIGENCE SUMMARY.
(Erase heading not required.)

Army Form C. 2118.

38th Div Ambulance Workshop.

Place	Date	Hour	Summary of Events and Information	Remarks and references to Appendices
LOCON	1-3-16		St David's Day, celebrated by the Division, message from G.O.C. Division issued in Divisional Orders. Reported that German Aeroplane brought down near Mes Plouse. Pt Bicknell returned to duty from leave. 2 Ford Ambulances in Shops. Received from D.D. of S.&T. pro forma for Petrol Consumption return.	
"	2-3-16		German Aeroplane dropped bomb in field near LOCON, reported to have been brought down soon afterwards. Men attended Concert given by Lena Ashwell's Concert Party. Received D.of T. Circular Memorandum No 143 re pistons & cylinders of Wolseley Cars. 2 Ford Ambulances in Shops.	
"	3-3-16		Received D of T Circular Memorandum No 142 re procedure when Lorries are sent to be re-tyred. 2 Ford Ambulances in Shops.	"
	4-3-16		Heavy fall of Snow. Transferred a few stores & spare parts to 38th Div Supply Column. Rendered to D.D. of S.&T. Petrol Consumption report. Sanitary Section Lorry ditched near Lestrem, breakdown lorry went out & brought Lorry in. 2 Ford Ambulances in Shops.	
	5-3-16		Issued new P.H. Smoke Helmets to men. Weather unsettled. 2 Ford Ambulances in Shops. 1 Wolseley Amb. 2 Motor Cycles.	

WAR DIARY or INTELLIGENCE SUMMARY.

Army Form C. 2118.

38th Div. Ambulance Workshop.

Place	Date	Hour	Summary of Events and Information	Remarks and references to Appendices
LOCON.	6-3-16		Fall of snow in the morning. Received Operation Orders No 7 from A.D.M.S re movement of Ambulances. Concert held in Div Recreation Room by the 14th Welsh Battalion. 2 Ford Ambs in shops 1 Wolseley Amb. 1 Sunbeam Amb. 3 Motor Cycles.	
"	7-3-16		Workshop DAIMLER LORRY broke down for first time since June 1915 with magneto trouble. Ambs in Shops 2 Fords 2 Motor Cycles.	
"	8-3-16		Heavy fall of snow. Ambs in Shops: 2 Fords 2 Wolseleys 3 Motor cycles.	
"	9-3-16		Number of British passed over on a raiding expedition. Letter from D.D of S+T re returning old sparking plugs to Base. Ambs in Shops: 2 Fords 2 Wolseley 2 Motor cycles.	
"	10-3-16		Received Operation Order No 8 from A.D.M.S. Read letter from D.D of S+T re lubricating oil for American Lorries. Memo from Div Hd. Qrs re Officers & Men in possession of Cameras. Ambs in Shops: 2 Fords. 1 Motor Cycle.	
"	11-3-16		Nothing of note to record. Ambs in Shops 2 Fords. 3 Wolseleys 1 Sunbeam 1 Motor Cycle.	
"	12-3-16		Very warm sunny weather. Rifles + equipment issued to men.	

WAR DIARY or INTELLIGENCE SUMMARY.

Army Form C. 2118.

(Erase heading not required.) 38th Div Ambulance Workshop.

Place	Date	Hour	Summary of Events and Information	Remarks and references to Appendices
LOCON	12-3-16		Recd Army Council Memorandum No 495 of 1916 re Cash Balances. Amb in Shop: 2 Fords 2 Wolseleys 1 Sunbeam. 2 Motor Cycles.	
"	13-3-16		Nothing of note to record. Amb in Shop: 2 Fords 2 Wolseleys 2 Motor Cycles.	
"	14-3-16		Recd Orders from A.S.C. Section at the Base to send home 102841 P/Cpl BURNS J. to base to be re-classified as a fitter. Recd Army Council Instructions No 500 of 1916. Amb in Shop: 2 Fords 3 Wolseleys 1 Sunbeam 2 Motor Cycles.	
"	15-3-16		Recd Wire from O.C. M.T. Base Depot that 1 fitter had been despatched as a reinforcement. To M/T 07382 Pte New F. taken on the strength as fitter. Recd letter from Div H.Qrs re Court Martials on cases of drunkenness. Amb in Shop: 2 Fords. 1 Wolseley. 2 Motor Cycles.	
"	16-3-16		Recd II Corps Administrative Orders. Amb in Shop: 2 Fords. 1 Wolseley 3 Motor Cycles.	
"	17-3-16		WOLSELEY Amb broke down between Lillers & Chocques, fitter sent to repair same. Recd letter from A.D.M.S. asking for number of Motor Ambulances not fitted with Electric Interior Lighting. Amb in Shop: 1 Ford 4 Wolseleys. 3 Motor Cycles.	
"	18-3-16		Recd Operation Order from A.D.M.S. Amb in Shop 1 Ford. 3 Wolseleys. 1 Motor Cycle.	

WAR DIARY or INTELLIGENCE SUMMARY.

38th Divl Ambulance Workshop.

Army Form C. 2118.

Place	Date	Hour	Summary of Events and Information	Remarks and references to Appendices
LOCON	19-3-16		Rec memorandum from A.S.C. Section at the Base to send in nominal Roll of M.T. drivers who could be classified as fitters. Ambs in Shops: 1 Ford 2 Wolseleys 2 Motor Cycles.	
"	20-3-16		Letter received from A.D.M.S. that Operation Order is suspended for 48 hours. Recd memo from D.D. of S.&T. re N.C.O's doing work when sent to the Heavy Repair Shop & instructions re same. Ambs in Shops: 1 Ford 3 Wolseleys. 1 Motor Cycle.	
"	21-3-16		M2/4128 M.SS. Brown H. proceeded on leave also M2/080949 Pte Webb J. Ambs in Shops: 1 Ford 3 Wolseleys. 1 Motor Cycle.	
"	22-3-16		Recd Memo from D.D. of S.&T. re N.C.O's & Men meaning M.T. fitters being irregular & calling for a return. Ambs in Workshop. 1 Ford 3 Wolseley 1 Motor Cycle.	
"	23-3-16		M2/073591 Cpl Bose. E.S. and M2/097274 Pte Cavanagh E. proceeded on leave. Recd from Paymaster re Clearing memo re Imprest a/c of January. Ambs in Shops: Ford 1. Wolseley 1. 1 Motor Cycle.	
"	24-3-16		Heavy Snowfall. Ambs in Shops. Ford 1. Wolseley 1. Motor Cycles 3.	
"	25-3-16		Car from Guards Division brought into shop with Worm wheel stripped. Ambs in Shops: Ford 1. Wolseley 1. Motor Cycles 3.	

WAR DIARY
or
INTELLIGENCE SUMMARY.
(Erase heading not required.)

Army Form C. 2118.

38th Div Ambulance Workshop.

Instructions regarding War Diaries and Intelligence Summaries are contained in F. S. Regs., Part II. and the Staff Manual respectively. Title pages will be prepared in manuscript.

Place	Date	Hour	Summary of Events and Information	Remarks and references to Appendices
LOCON	26-3-16		Nothing of note to record. Amb in Shops: Ford 1. Wolseleys 2. Motor Cycles 3.	
"	27-3-16		Nothing of note to record. Amb in Shops: Ford 1. Wolseley 2. Motor Cycles 4.	
"	28-3-16		Red D of T Circular re Older men for Administrative Services. Amb in Shops Ford 1. Wolseleys 2. Motor Cycles 4.	
"	29-3-16		M.S.S. Brown H. and Pt Webb G. returned to duty from leave. Amb in Shops: Ford 2. Wolseleys 3. Motor Cycles 3.	
"	30-3-16		Received G.R.O. 1484 re Div Ambulance Workshop being abolished and the whole of personnel & Vehicles being transferred to Div Supply Column. One Lorry and one Car with 3 drivers to be evacuated under instructions for the D of T. Amb in Shops: Fords 2. Wolseleys 3.	
"	31-3-16		Recd from A.S.C. Section Base circular memo calling for Nominal Roll of A.S.C. Warrant Officers & N.C.O.s including acting rank. Amb in Workshop: Fords 2. Motor Cycles 1.	

E. H. Lambert Lt A.S.C.
O.C. 38th Div Ambulance Workshop.